Thomas E. Dewey
on the Two-Party System

By John A. Wells

THE VOTER'S PRESIDENTIAL HANDBOOK—1960

Thomas E. Dewey
on the Two-Party System

Edited and with a Foreword
by John A. Wells

Doubleday & Company, Inc., Garden City, New York, 1966

Excerpts from *The Taft Story*, by William S. White, reprinted by permission of Harper & Row, Publishers.

Library of Congress Catalog Card Number 65–19936
Copyright © 1966 by John A. Wells
All Rights Reserved
Printed in the United States of America
First Edition

Foreword

It is unusual for an active and prominent political figure to present his considered views on the American political system. Politicians tend to be activists—practical men. They may write articles or books on given issues, they may write memoirs, but they leave the theory of working politics to academic observers.

Early in 1950, while serving in the eighth year of twelve years as Governor of New York, Thomas E. Dewey delivered a series of lectures at Princeton University on the American political system—what makes it work and what are the major internal and external threats arrayed against it.*

The basic dangers which Governor Dewey saw and described so clearly—the decline of the two-party system, the steady gathering of political power in Washington at the expense of state and local governments, a complacent and

---

* At that time he gratefully acknowledged the collaboration given him in preparation of the lectures by Mr. Gabriel Hauge, later Economic Adviser to President Eisenhower.

v

at times unrealistic foreign policy—have since grown to ominous proportions.

Except for quotations in contemporary newspapers these lectures were never published. Last year I suggested to Governor Dewey that his lectures were sharply pertinent to a number of crucial problems the nation, the two-party system and the Republican party then faced and would undoubtedly continue to face in the future. I asked his permission to publish them. The Governor agreed, and the lectures are presented herewith as originally delivered, subject to minor editing necessary for publication and the omission of topical material.

What Governor Dewey has to say on the two-party system is, if possible, even more applicable today. Protection of our fundamental political liberty depends on two parties with reasonably equal strength, and that means the Republican party must be broad-based, moderate, and forward-looking. Both parties should stand for the same general principles and objectives, differing, of course, in matters of degree and on the all-important means of achieving these common goals. Only in this way can full public confidence be maintained, and disruptive upheavals be avoided following a change in administrations. In these lectures Governor Dewey disposes of the recurring suggestion that the parties be "realigned":

> Let me return to the basic fact that both parties include people of all walks of life and station, that today neither party is sectional, and that they are alike in most of their stated objectives. It is only necessary to compare the platforms of both parties in a normal presidential year to find

how similar they are. This similarity is highly objectionable to a vociferous few. They rail at both parties, saying they represent nothing but a choice between Tweedledee and Tweedledum. I must say that I have most often heard this view expressed by people who have no experience in government and are either extreme reactionaries or radicals who want a neat little party to carry out their special prejudices; or these people are pseudo-intellectuals or just plain obstructionists. None of them contributes much to the sober, tough business of modern government.

These impractical theorists with a "passion for neatness" demand that our parties be sharply divided, one against the other, in interest, membership, and doctrine. They want to drive all moderates and liberals out of the Republican party and then have the remainder join forces with the conservative groups of the South. Then they would have everything very neatly arranged, indeed. The Democratic party would be the liberal-to-radical party. The Republican party would be the conservative-to-reactionary party.

The results would be neatly arranged, too. The Republicans would lose every election and the Democrats would win every election. It may be a perfect theory, but it would result in a one-party system and finally in totalitarian government. As you may suspect by now, I am against it.

Governor Dewey's discussion is not only pertinent to the perennial warfare between our two great parties. Much of it is directly relevant to the continuing struggles between moderate-liberals and the conservatives of the Republican party. He is particularly well qualified to speak out on behalf of the moderate-liberal wing of the Party.* For over a

* See appendix for a brief recapitulation of Governor Dewey's career.

decade he was the pre-eminent leader of this wing, while the late United States Senator Robert A. Taft was the acknowledged leader of the conservative wing.

William S. White has aptly described the positions of these two outstanding Republican leaders in his sympathetic and perceptive biography, *The Taft Story:*

> For thirteen years, from 1940 to his death in 1953, Robert A. Taft and Thomas E. Dewey stood as the two great protagonists of the two Republican parties of the United States. The history of all this period of Republicanism was in the practical sense the history of these two men. Their titanic struggles with each other symbolized two whole ways of political thought and political life.
>
> Taft represented, if not always exactly, a Republican party that was essentially old-fashioned, essentially isolationist, and had its hopes and policies based in the past. Dewey, with more exactness, represented a Republican party that was essentially forward-looking (Taft would have said spineless), dominantly internationalist, and willing as time went on to face one after another the realities of the political revolution Woodrow Wilson had started and Franklin Roosevelt had carried to full power . . .
>
> The Taft Republicans took the position that nothing the Democrats had done, or might do, could be of much good. The Dewey Republicans took the view that, both as a practical matter and as a principle, it was necessary to assess the New Deal and then the Fair Deal in detail to select what ought to be cast out. To Taft, in his political philosophy of either-or, this notion of the Deweyites was heretical. Worse, it was a kind of desertion in the face of the enemy.

It was the Dewey Republicans and other leaders of the moderate-liberal state Republican parties who made possible the nomination of General Eisenhower for President in 1952.

The practical, common-sense approach of the modern Republican moderate pervades Governor Dewey's discussion. Throughout, he emphasizes the importance of the continuing quest for workable solutions to the foreign and domestic problems which the United States faces, and his discussion of the principles and conduct of foreign policy is as valid today as it was sixteen years ago. All political moderates, regardless of party affiliation, will derive from these lectures much food for thought and many applications relevant to today's problems.

These lectures by an experienced, intelligent, national political leader show how little real change sixteen years has seen in the basic problems of the Cold War, the continuing struggle between the Democratic and the Republican parties, and the conflict between the moderate-liberal and the conservative wings of the Republican party.

Governor Dewey did not wish to participate in any royalties resulting from this book. He did suggest that Princeton University had supplied the forum for the lectures and should receive an appropriate portion of the royalties. This has been arranged.

John A. Wells

New York City
1966

*This book is dedicated to
the thousands of men and women who,
at great personal sacrifice, maintain the
vigor of our two national political parties.*

I

The Two-Party System

Although the United States is the youngest of the great nations, ours is one of the oldest free republics on earth. Its durability has persisted in the face of wars and the inevitable frailty of human beings who conduct government. Our nation is the principal support of the free world today. It remains, after a century and three-quarters, the inspiration for the basic concepts of liberty everywhere.

Today that moral leadership is under sharp challenge by the leaders of the new totalitarian ideology of the left, who even challenge our right to exist. They insist that Communism cannot live in the same world with individual freedom. They publicly insist that their system shall survive and that ours shall not. Under these circumstances, it seems to me particularly important that we re-examine the wellsprings of our liberties and the political system by which we keep them.

At the outset let me confess that I am a biased witness.

My political bias as a Republican is obvious. But there is a much more important principle at stake today. I believe with all my soul that government exists for the primary purpose of securing human liberty. I believe that every other purpose is subordinate to this one and I regard with scorn and contempt all those who would sell human rights for a mess of governmental pottage.

In addition to the explicit guarantees of the Bill of Rights, I believe that liberty includes equal opportunity for all, regardless of race, color or creed, the right to own property, the right to seek or reject employment, the right to think and create. I believe that each individual human being has a right to rise to the fullest, material, intellectual and spiritual achievements of which he is capable. I believe government exists to preserve these rights and opportunities to the fullest extent that their enjoyment does not deprive others of their similar rights.

I also believe that twentieth-century free government can still protect all of these rights while meeting the problems of personal security and economic stability in an industrial age.

This statement of fundamental principles will not appeal to anyone who accepts the chopped-down, bobtailed versions of our liberties which are peddled by followers of Karl Marx and their fellow travelers. But I have observed no changes in human nature or in governments which have repealed the Biblical exaltation of the importance of the individual human soul or the traditional liberal faith that human rights transcend all other values.

The Constitution of the United States, of course, is the

basis for our free system. But other countries have had excellent constitutions, both written and unwritten. Other nations, too, have enjoyed great land areas, rich in minerals and productivity. Many of these nations have risen and fallen, some of them several times, during the life of our country. So, it is not alone the Constitution or our natural resources which has made possible our unparalleled success as a nation and the preservation of the freedom we enjoy.

We must find the rest of the answer elsewhere. In my view, it lies in the American political system which grew up under but outside our Constitution. This lecture is an inquiry into the nature of that political system.

2

Our political history has been the story of a two-party system in action. From the early days of the Republic our basic political arrangement has been the same—one party in power and one party in opposition. Within this alignment we have built and operated our system of government. Any inquiry into the American political scene should begin with this central fact.

If the American two-party system had not existed, we should have invented it. In fact, that is exactly what we did.

The men who declared and won our independence, who formed first the Confederation and later framed the Constitution, did not expect the development of political parties. Political parties were regarded with suspicion as leading to factionalism, passion, and intrigue. James Madison, for example, believed that public issues would be decided by majorities composed of passing combinations of groups and interests.

Nevertheless, by George Washington's second term as President a two-party system had already appeared in the groups led by Alexander Hamilton and Thomas Jefferson. While it would be fascinating to discuss the history of American party politics, my purpose here is to emphasize the wisdom of the choice we have made in developing two alternative political parties as a guarantee of popular sovereignty and of political responsibility.

There are other methods of choosing governments. One of them is the one-party system. It prevails in Russia and all her satellites today, as it did in pre-war Nazi Germany and in Fascist Italy. The Nazis were a minority party when Adolf Hitler became Chancellor of Germany and seized full power. It is said that in 1917 it took only 30,000 Communists to seize the reins of government in all Russia, with its 145,000,000 people. Certainly there were comparatively few real Communists in China or in the Central European countries which are now ruled by Communists.

Under the Communist one-party system its small membership is organized and disciplined. It confers upon itself by decree a monopoly of effective political action. Absolute civil as well as military power is vested in leadership which also enjoys a monopoly of political propaganda. Blind acceptance of party dogma is enforced upon all the people. Deviation is swiftly followed by the concentration camp or the firing squad. There have not been many successful internal revolutions in modern times against an established one-party government backed up by the machine guns, tanks and airplanes of armed forces under iron party control.

Even in a free country it is difficult to oust an entrenched leadership. Whether you are a member of a labor union, a stockholder in a business corporation or a member of any other organized group, it is very difficult for you to get rid of the "ins."

So long as we keep both of our political parties healthy we need never suffer the disaster of one-party government in America. We have the priceless constitutional guarantee that we may on fixed dates, known years in advance, throw out any national administration we do not like. The same guarantees exist with respect to state and local governments. The only danger nationally has been that one party might become too strong, or able to use the enormous new powers of government to perpetuate itself in office, as is the case in politically lop-sided, machine-dominated cities or in the "Solid South." Even in these circumstances, the dominant party has frequently split and free elections have made change possible.

In contrast to the one-party system, several European countries have six or eight or more political parties representing various religious, racial, economic or class alignments. In conversation with the Premier of one European nation some years ago, he said that, second only to the Communists, the greatest curse of his government was that he had to work with twenty-six political parties.

5

When there are more than two major parties, no one party can ordinarily expect a majority. Every government, therefore, becomes a coalition. On almost every issue that arises one section of the coalition may break off and the government may then lose its parliamentary majority. It is difficult and often impossible for the government to plan its course, even for as long as from month to month. This system produces great instability. After each election or resignation of a cabinet, a new government must be formed and again there are frenzied intrigues among the parties in working out the next coalition.

A member of a European parliament—a former Premier —once told me, with considerable relish, that he expected to control the action of his government on the budget which was then coming up. He said, with a smile, that he could control sixty votes in opposition though he could only deliver twenty votes in favor. But his sixty votes, out of more than five hundred members, were enough to give him the whip hand, though he was not the leader of any party and had received no popular support at the polls for government leadership. This illustrates how minority groups which join a government have a power far beyond their popular support. Often they are in a position to blackjack the major parties who have the responsibility of keeping a coalition government functioning. This is a fundamental violation of the principle of majority rule as well as the essentials of responsible government.

Here, under our two-party system we have few of the instabilities of the multi-party system, though we do

6

achieve our own kind of coalitions. We make our coalitions within the parties and instead of achieving them after election, we make them before election. Every four years the national conventions of the two parties present sharp controversies. Sometimes the fights over party platforms are taken to the floor and the debates as well as the votes are close and bitter. There are often some who "take a walk" from the convention, either publicly or quietly. But finally candidates for President and Vice-President are nominated, a platform is adopted and the party then goes on to fight the election.

Why do the parties have these bitter internal fights? And why must they achieve their own coalitions? Because there are wide divergencies of opinion in each of the two great parties. And why are there these wide divergencies of opinion? Because each party really represents a composite spectrum of roughly similar interests. Each contains farmers; each contains industrial workers; each includes businessmen and scholars; each attracts men and women from every walk and station of life. No single religion or color or race or economic interest is confined to one or the other of our parties. Each party is to some extent a reflection of the other.

The result is that since the Civil War the parties have not been too far apart on most fundamentals of our system. This means that the choice of one or the other party during this period has not represented anything like a revolution or, in the past at least, a threat to the basic institutions and interests of our people. It has meant also, and

7

this is perhaps part of the secret of our enormous economic power in the world, that a change from one party to the other has usually involved a continuity of action and policy of the nation as a whole on most fundamentals.

A free economy is the total of the decisions of individual enterprises—farmers, shopkeepers, industrialists, bankers, and others. It is a sensitive mechanism, too, and the shock of major change in either direction after a political election would do great damage to the people's welfare. This is only one of the reasons why, as a people, we have learned to distrust and avoid extremes of principles and of interests in our public life. When the Democratic party forgot this mandate for national unity and became sectional, it caused the tragedy of secession and the agony of civil war.

Let me return to the basic fact that both parties include people of all walks of life and station, that today neither party is sectional and that they are alike in most of their stated objectives. It is only necessary to compare the platforms of both parties in a normal presidential year to find how similar they are. This similarity is highly objectionable to a vociferous few. They rail at both parties, saying they represent nothing but a choice between Tweedledee and Tweedledum. I must say that I have most often heard this view expressed by people who have no experience in government and are either extreme reactionaries or radicals who want a neat little party to carry out their special prejudices; or these people are pseudo-intellectuals or just plain obstructionists. None of them contributes much to the sober, tough business of modern government.

8

These impractical theorists with a "passion for neatness" demand that our parties be sharply divided, one against the other, in interest, membership, and doctrine. They want to drive all moderates and liberals out of the Republican party and then have the remainder join forces with the conservative groups of the South. Then they would have everything very neatly arranged, indeed. The Democratic party would be the liberal-to-radical party. The Republican party would be the conservative-to-reactionary party.

The results would be neatly arranged, too. The Republicans would lose every election and the Democrats would win every election. It may be a perfect theory but it would result in a one-party system and finally totalitarian government. As you may suspect by now, I am against it.

The resemblance between the parties and the similarities which their party platforms show are the very heart of the strength of the American political system. We are, in truth, all members of the same family. The disparaging epithets of those who want everything clear-cut and simple cannot erase the stubborn fact that our objectives and interests as Americans are not neatly opposed but are, and I hope always will be, mutual.

Lest anyone misunderstand, let me say that there remains a broad and inviting battleground over which the two parties can vigorously contend. I shall return to that enticing subject often in this series of lectures.

For more than a century and a half the two-party system has served our country well. Thus far we have survived every kind of crisis. We are still the strongest nation on earth. We have preserved our liberties. As against the single party or the multi-party system, I think it is clear that our two-party tradition, despite occasional failures, has been the most effective instrument of government yet devised and should be vigorously supported.

3

Now is there a legitimate role for third parties in this country? The answer depends on whether the third party is national in character with intellectual breadth and a broad base of popular support or whether it is narrowly local in nature.

Such sectional or local parties are, basically, only splinter movements. They have proved to be a menace to responsible government here just as they have to free governments elsewhere. I see no useful place for them in a free system such as ours.

We do not have to travel farther from Princeton than across the Hudson River into New York State to find plenty of examples. In the 1948 presidential election there were seven parties on the voting machines—the Republican, Democratic, Liberal, American Labor, Socialist, Industrial Government, and Socialist Worker. Only the Republicans and Democrats were truly national parties. Even Henry Wallace, the candidate of the Progressive party, was on the ballot in only part of the states.

Two of these minority groups have a substantial following and are really splinter parties. One is the so-called American Labor party* which since early in 1944 has been a Communist front. It has been universally recognized as such. Despite this fact Democratic state-wide candidates accepted its nomination as recently as 1946.

The other splinter group is the so-called Liberal party, a faction which broke off from the American Labor party when the Communists took it over in 1944.

Both of these splinter parties are operated at large expense, principally out of the pockets of union members for purposes of political bargaining and personal aggrandizement of a few leaders.

The Democratic party in New York State today can hardly expect to win any state-wide election without the support of the Liberal party. Every state-wide election, beginning in 1938, demonstrated that the New York Democratic party is a prisoner of its alliances. In each of those elections Democratic state-wide candidates received the support of one or both of the then-major splinter parties. In the years when they won, it was the votes contributed by the splinter parties which provided the margin of victory. Here is a dramatic demonstration of the danger of splinter parties, and, also, of one of the ways in which an old party can lose its independence as well as its character.

By contrast with local or sectional splinters, genuine,

* This party has now passed out of existence. A new state-wide splinter party is the Conservative party, which represents a narrow, rightist point of view. J.A.W.

nation-wide third party movements have, at times, served a real purpose during our history. All organizations, and most particularly political organizations, tend to become stuffy and ingrown. They become reluctant to take risks or accept change. All too often they do not welcome new-comers to their ranks for fear those holding secure leader-ship on a narrow base will lose it to new individuals or groups. One thing is certain, when both parties ignore the rise of new issues, new parties come into being.

Nothing rouses a politician so much as a lot of votes going some place else. When that happens, one and often both of the older parties will embrace and absorb the new issues and the new cause.

History records that the chief political divisions of the Eastern Roman Empire were based on chariot racing, with the factions of the Blues and Greens in the Circus domi-nating political life. Heaven forbid that American political divisions should be based on the Yankees vs. the Dodgers, Notre Dame vs. the Army, or even Yale vs. Princeton!

We have been delivered from this fate by the various na-tional third parties which have risen from time to time. This is their role—not to continue as an instrument of pri-vate, sectional, class or group power. Their role has been to rise up, teach a lesson and either take over one of the two great parties or be absorbed into it. This they have done, teaching the old parties that to live and retain office they must change with changing times. Change is the law of life. It is death to resist it.

12

4

How, then, does change come about? To find the answer, we must first inquire into the true nature of the two major political parties. Everybody talks about them, likes or dislikes them, and most people damn one and support the other. But is the true nature of the parties understood, even by all of their leaders? I doubt it. I will go further and pose the question: In the sense of a unified organization with a national viewpoint on major issues, does either party exist at all? I will go still further and ask: Is there such a thing as a national Democratic party or a national Republican party?

From long observation and active participation, I have reached a solemn conclusion which I have hitherto kept to myself. I think this is a good time to let you in on the secret.

I seriously doubt whether in this sense there is a genuine national party of either name.

The first obvious fact is that each party has its base in the individual states. One of the pillars of the two-party system is the fact that we have ninety-six [now one hundred] parties, one Democratic party and one Republican party in each of the forty-eight [now fifty] states.

All of the forms of genuine national parties exist but the substance is very shadowy. One party has a President in office so people think they can judge what that party stands for by his actions. They rarely read the party platform and if the members of the Congress of the President's party do not go along with him, the average citizen just writes it off to cussedness or the lobbyists. The press encourages this illusion by cartooning the Congress as an ignorant, muddle-headed, lazy fellow.

Who speaks for the party out of power? It has its last nominee for President who is called the "Titular Head of the Party." I have held that title in my party now for nearly six years and I still have some doubts about what it means except that I am the last, duly nominated spokesman for my party.

There are others who also speak for the party out of power. There is the National Committee, with two elected representatives from each state. It is represented by a National Chairman in Washington, D.C. He purports to speak for his party.

Then there are the members of the House and the Senate of the party out of power. I know from close experience that many of them believe that they are the sole and only trustees of party policy. Here the difficulty is that they are seldom unanimous and they sometimes appear to vote contrary to the platform adopted at their last national convention.

In the final analysis one is forced to the conclusion that each party reflects the opinions of millions of people and of hundreds of leaders. Every thoughtful person will find men who represent his particular views in both parties. He will also find men in both parties who represent practically everything he disagrees with. The total of a party is the total opinion of many people. It changes constantly. It is

never wholly represented by one man even when he is
President. Often a party majority opinion is actually mis-
represented by the minority or the wrong-headed who are
the loudest and get the most headlines.

If you want to judge the two parties—and I think this is
of critical importance—you should judge them by what
they do when they are in power, not by what they do when
they are in the opposition. By this I mean that you can
judge a party best only when it has control of both the executive and the legislative branches of the national government.

On this basis it is easy to judge the present Democratic
party for the things it has done and failed to do, the progress it has made and the kind of administration it has given
while it has been in power. I assume you will like many of
the things it has done and dislike many of its domestic and
foreign policy failures.

You might try to judge the Republican party by the way
its various members in the House of Representatives and
the Senate have voted on individual issues. One difficulty
with this is that the minority is rarely able to vote on a bill
which it has drawn itself. It has to vote on bills prepared
by the majority, often sent over from the White House.
The minority may believe in every objective of those bills
but find them offensive in bad draftsmanship, in loose or
self-defeating provisions, or in the granting of excessive
power to the Executive.

Usually the minority is not allowed to rewrite a bill and
cure its defects. So, able and honorable men are often
impelled to vote against bills of whose objectives they

approve, risking the wrath of their constituents and mis-representation of their motives, in order to avoid the evils of making progress backward.

On rare occasions the minority can bring over enough members of the majority in order to rewrite a bad bill and achieve the good objective. An example of this occurred just last year [in 1949] when the very important bill providing arms for Europe came over to the Senate from the White House. It was so bad in the granting of grossly excessive powers to the Executive and in its wasteful financial pro-visions that men of strong internationalist viewpoints, like Senators Vandenberg and Dulles, were unable to support it. These two Senators were able to persuade enough mem-bers of the majority to agree with them so that they were able to rewrite the bill. In doing so they probably saved the bill from defeat and certainly saved the country from a grave usurpation of power by the Executive and great waste of public moneys.

It is not often that the minority can rewrite an impossi-ble bill with good objectives to make it supportable. The result is that you can rarely judge a party by the way it votes when it is in the minority. You can only judge it by what it does when it is in control of government, either na-tional or state, or by its party platform.

I once reviewed the platforms of the Republican party adopted in 1936, 1940, 1944, and 1948. Over the twelve-year period they were generally consistent declarations of forward-looking, constructive leadership. They were a fair statement of what over a thousand delegates—men and women from all over the country—declared their Republicanism to mean in each of those four conventions. The declarations were strong, progressive, and positive.

It is quite true that the Republican appeal to the country in these years failed. I have my own theories as to why, as I am sure you do. But in my analysis of those Republican campaigns the message and spirit of the platforms were an asset, not a liability.

One of the great elements of strength in our two-party system lies in the forty-eight [now fifty] Republican and forty-eight [now fifty] Democratic parties in the United States. They cut across every sectional and group and class line. The unit of the party is in the state. This means that in years of Democratic national predominance, state and local Republican parties and officials retain power, keep their organizations alive and provide the bases for future national success.

Each individual state provides a vital base for the two-party system, surrounded by durable levees which usually resist the flood of national majorities and the pressure of national politics. A constant flow of new ideas and new leadership keeps coming up from the ranks in local and state governments. As a result neither party can be destroyed by the national victories of the other but only by becoming sectional, reactionary or ingrown.

5

From time to time in our history, one party or the other has enjoyed a long period of ascendancy because it has

17

grasped an opportunity or because the other party has mis-calculated.

Such a period began in 1800, when Jefferson grasped the essential fact that popular government was to be the rule of American politics after the Federalists had failed to perceive that the eighteenth century was over. Despite occasional interruptions by Federalists and Whigs, it was not until 1860 that there was a basic shift in party control.

Here was a time when a third party came into being—new, national and inspired with high purpose. The Federalists and the Whigs, having failed to meet the burning issues of the day, disappeared.

With Lincoln's election, the Republican era began and endured, with only three interruptions by Democratic administrations, for over seventy years. The source of the weakness of the Democrats was their fatal dream of an agrarian society based, historically, on the institution of human slavery. The source of Republican power was its emphasis on personal freedom and its acceptance of the implications of the Industrial Revolution.

The check to this Republican period came in 1932, following the financial panic and business depression. Of course, this was a world-wide collapse but since it came during a Republican administration, it was blamed on the Republican party. People naturally blame the party in power when things go badly and give it credit when things go well. It is a basic instinct which leads a political leader to be absent when the news is bad and to be in the center of the stage taking the applause for good news.

It is too late to debate the various expedients by which

the series of Democratic administrations since 1932 have attempted to make the Great Depression the basis for a self-perpetuating vote-getting system. At this point, we need only note that the process has been accompanied by tremendous Federal centralization, massive spending, greatly expanded bureaucracy, and debt, high taxes, and high prices, and by widely increased regulation of the individual. Certainly much good has been done and certainly some harm.

When these encroachments will lead to a popular revulsion against the Democratic party I do not know. We do know that similar encroachments in Australia and New Zealand have in the past led to the overthrow of strongly entrenched socialist governments and to the effective restoration of what is basically a two-party system in those distant British commonwealths.

These defeats of labor governments have been hailed with immense enthusiasm by most Republicans and many Democrats. They can easily be misunderstood, however. Both in New Zealand and Australia, the successful parties, like the Republican party in its national campaigns since 1936, assured the people that they proposed to retain the welfare provisions made by their opponents. Those elections provide no comfort for those in either party who think they are going to win any elections on a platform of back-to-Methuselah. Those elections were not won except upon the firmest assurances that the social clock would not be turned back.

In Great Britain the Conservatives similarly assured the people that they would not repeal their social security. Mr.

Churchill went further and vigorously pointed out that the entire welfare program adopted by the Labour Government was conceived, had its period of gestation, and was delivered by a committee appointed by him as Prime Minister. In short, the Conservatives took the credit for the social program and promised to do it better. Whatever our view of the wisdom of these decisions, they do represent the judgment of exceedingly able political leaders in other English-speaking nations. Even under the parliamentary system, the opposition cannot save the country unless it wins the election.

All this is instructive for the Republican party. It is still in the wilderness today after four unsuccessful attempts to regain national power. Each of those attempts [as of 1950] was based upon a liberal platform and led by a candidate who assured the people that he did not intend to repeal the twentieth century. Because of this there are some loud voices in the Republican party denouncing all the platforms and nominees with the epithet "me too." The complaint and the epithet largely originated with those who hold isolationist or extremely conservative views, or both.

As for myself, and I believe most of the members of the Republican party, we refuse to be against the Ten Commandments just because the Democrats say they are for them. I also refuse to be against sound government action supporting such basic modern concepts as collective bargaining, minimum wages, unemployment insurance, regulation of markets for capital, old age insurance, or equal rights for all regardless of race, color, creed, or national origin. We in New York State led the nation in breaking down barriers of religious and racial discrimination in employment. Just because the Democrats then came along and said they also were for it, is no reason for the Republican party to turn against it to avoid the epithet "me too."

I believe Republicans generally will refuse to be intimidated or confused by the epithet "me too." Our party has a great tradition of sound, progressive leadership in the interests of all the people. It would be a catastrophe if it should falter now and listen to the croaking voices of reaction or isolation. Then the party might really become what the Democrats call it. Then it would have an attitude of complete negativism which all history shows is the beginning of political rigor mortis.

6

In a two-party system the vigor of each party is indispensable. The Democratic party has held national power most of the time since 1932. The Republicans having been in opposition for such a long period, it is not unnatural that the vital traditions of the party should have been forgotten by many, including many Republicans. If we are to restore the strength of the two-party system, the vigorous Republican tradition must be reasserted.

A great realignment of the American two-party system was foreshadowed by the inability of the Whigs to face up to the issue of slavery. The Kansas-Nebraska Act of 1854 broke that party asunder. All through the North and West there surged a mighty tide of sentiment against the institution of human bondage.

The Republican party arose to express this great new political sentiment. It was the third party to bear that name. Jefferson's Republican-Democratic party stood for individual liberty even to the point of endangering law and order. This basic principle of individual liberty was lost to the Democratic party when the Republicans took their stand firmly upon the exclusion of slavery from the new lands of the West and its inevitable abolition from all the States of the Union. In a letter he wrote to a Boston committee in 1859 for a Jefferson birthday festival, Lincoln pronounced himself a thorough disciple of Jefferson and found in the principles of Jefferson "the definitions and axioms of a free society."

The accent of the new party was on freedom. In its first national campaign in 1856, the slogan was, "Free labor, free speech, free men, free Kansas and Fremont." It was a party conceived in that spirit that preserved the Union. As I have previously said, during fifty-six of the seventy-two years from 1860 to 1932, the people sent Republicans to the White House.

Over the course of those decades, the United States completed the opening up of her vast continent and grew in population and wealth until she was the wonder of the world. Blessed with rich natural resources and a temperate climate, the industry and genius of her people prospered under this system of personal freedom. Men and women from all over the world came to our shores to seek their fortunes and live out their lives in freedom. For here was the great new world where a man could work out his own destiny, free from the cloying hand of arbitrary government and the barriers of a class society. Here his talents might have full release, and he could become what he was capable of becoming. Here there was reward for effort and opportunity for all.

To the building of this society the Republican party contributed the essential framework of government. It was a framework based on personal freedom with both a moral and a pragmatic sanction. It had behind it the tremendous moral drive that raised the yoke of slavery from the necks of four million human beings in this country. It provided the means for turning loose the genius of our people to seize the opportunities the Industrial Revolution made possible. To the emphasis of the Democratic party on the agrarian life, the Republican party added a vital interest in the mines and the factories and in finance. Thus it fostered the creation of the industrial capital and the tools that would raise the standard of life of our people and make our country strong in the family of nations.

The Republican party's determination to make our country a land of opportunity for all was evidenced by the promise of free land in the Republican platform of 1860. This pledge was redeemed in 1862 when Congress passed, and President Lincoln signed, the Homestead Act. This was one of the dramatic events of history. Over the years it peopled our vast and empty Western lands and accelerated the opening up of the continent.

To speed the development of the country the Republican party initiated legislation to foster the building of railway lines to the Pacific coast. This action accelerated the spanning of the continent. Markets and investment opportunities were multiplied. Those seeking land were benefited since it was easier to move West and stake out a claim for free land. The railroads brought back the agricultural products to Eastern markets thereby feeding the East and increasing the value of the farm homesteads.

The use of the powers of government to aid in developing our resources through the initiative of the people is in the Republican tradition.

Today, when the value of the dollar has been steadily reduced, it is well to remember that the Republican party from the beginning has fought to give the country sound money. From the Democratic administrations preceding its accession to power in 1860, it inherited a system of "wildcat" banking and depreciated bank notes. To cope with financial disorders and to help the sale of bonds, Congress established the national banking system in 1863. Later, against the Greenbackers and again against William Jennings Bryan, the Republicans fought and won the battle for a sound dollar. That battle is again upon us and is a rising threat to the stability of the nation.

The growth of big business organizations after the Civil War led to a concern over the rise of monopoly power. In 1890, Republican Senator John Sherman of Ohio sponsored and secured passage of the Anti-Trust Act bearing his name. This was the first national action to forbid trusts and combinations in restraint of trade and it imposed penalties for violation.

It was a Republican President who launched the federal

24

conservation policy in 1891 and it was Theodore Roosevelt who extended this policy widely and vigorously. Other social advances which were major victories in their time included the Pure Food and Drug Act of 1906, the Railway Labor Mediation Act of 1926, President Coolidge's support in 1927 of the Congressional resolution favoring a Child Labor Amendment and President Hoover's signing of the Norris-La Guardia Act in 1932.

Others would include establishment of the Civil Service Commission in 1883, the record of President Taft in supporting the income tax amendment to the Constitution and his long, successful fight for the establishment of a parcel post and of a postal savings system. All these may seem commonplace today but they were great, progressive advances in their time and were achieved only in the face of bitter opposition.

In the field of foreign policy, Republican administrations established and advanced our position in the world and, even in opposition, the party has made remarkable contributions.

There are, of course, many faults in the record. No party could rule a nation for most of seventy-two years without making blunders. The oppression and corruption in the South which followed the assassination of Abraham Lincoln were inexcusable. Incidentally, it set back the two-party system so far in the South that only a vestige exists even today. There was corruption, notably in the Grant and the Harding administrations. There was also a failure to perceive the necessity of revising tariff policies when we changed from a debtor to a creditor nation.

No party fails to make blunders but, also, no party can win most of the national elections for seventy-two years unless it is vital, forward-looking, and constructively serves the needs of the people.

I have cited some of the Republican achievements to remind us all that the Republican record of administration is positive, not negative. There is none of the blind obstructionism which Democrats claim is our habit and some Republicans would like to take as our role.

7

The two-party system has provided our country with government under which it has made the mightiest progress in the history of the world. I have declared my fundamental belief that the highest purpose of government is to preserve human freedom. Our system has fulfilled that purpose.

Periodic change from the dominance of one party to the other preserves our habits and traditions of peaceful adjustment and brings fresh life and thinking to the problems of government.

The ferment in the party of opposition is significant because the party of opposition will in due course become the party in power. The nature of that ferment is decisive because it determines how soon the country will have a change and the direction it will then take.

Free nations do not go backward. They may abandon their follies but rarely their successes. The only way in which the opposition party can prepare itself to be recalled to power is by offering better solutions for the problems of the day than are offered by the party in office.

We must, of course, learn from the mistakes of the past. Even more we must learn from the achievements of the past. It was a wise man who said: "From the altar of the past take not the ashes but the fire."

II

Party Conflict and the Modern Dilemma

From the days of primitive tribal chieftains the one certainty about government has been the certainty of change. Whether it be progress or retrogression, change is the rule.

In the absolute monarchies of the past, change was achieved by the shifting of royal favorites, by the rise and fall of the king's prime minister and by the replacement of palace advisers. Quite often these changes were accompanied by violence. Confiscation of lands, exile, torture, and execution were common instruments for making the changes effective and dramatic.

In the Soviet Union and its satellites today the purge is both the instrument of change and the means of securing the leadership in undisputed control. In the 1930s when the Politburo decided to abandon the policy of collective security, Foreign Minister Litvinov and his associates disappeared from the scene and were replaced by Mr. Molotov and his group. The change in policy was immediate and effective.

When it was decided to enforce Marxist dogma in the

science of genetics, all the scholars in the field were gathered together to present their views. After all had made their opinions clear, those who believed in heredity disappeared. The Lysenko interpretation of Marxian philosophy that environment is all-important, became totally accepted. There were few scientists left in public view who disagreed.

When it was finally determined that the landowning kulaks must give way to complete collectivization of agriculture, millions of human beings were liquidated. This ended overt resistance to government policy.

1

Free government substitutes a conflict of parties for the more lethal methods used elsewhere.

Under the American system we make our changes through vigorous but essentially peaceful party conflict. Like the old definition of fox hunting, our politics resemble "war without its cruelty and only 90 percent of its danger."

As I have previously pointed out, the founders of our republic were suspicious of political parties as leading to factionalism, passion, and intrigue. They were quite right. But these defects are present in all governments and they have not prevented the two-party system from serving us well.

One of the reasons our system has been so successful in preserving liberty is that basically it provides a substitute for assassination, execution, purges, and violent popular uprisings. We get our political passions and factionalism right out in the open where everybody can see them. Even most of the intrigue, with the frequently unwanted help of the press, gets into the open. The result is that the people may become aroused and take action at the polls. Or they can laugh. But in any event, the steam is let off peaceably and without violence.

In spite of passing bitterness and occasional violence at the polls, I think it is safe to say that no great nation makes its political decisions in better temper or with a better will to accept the final verdict. This is a major achievement of our two-party system and a tribute to our national sanity and sense of humor.

It is symbolized, perhaps, by the fact that a defeated President or governor participates in the inauguration of his successor. Quite often a former leader of the opposition is called to one form of service or another by the party in office. In my own experience I appointed a defeated opponent to one public office and offered appointment to another.

Party conflict goes on continuously in the day-by-day, give-and-take of administration and opposition in the nation and in the states. It is conducted on the floor of the legislative assemblies, in the newspapers, on the television and radio and at public meetings. There is the constant contest between the parties to capture the public imagination, to capitalize on their own achievements and exploit the failures of the other side.

In this party warfare, Democrats generally work much harder at the daily business of politics than Republicans.

They have always seemed to me to be more reckless in their charges, more sweeping in their claims and more lavish in their promises—and much more effective in dramatizing their case.

By contrast Republicans tend to work harder at the exacting business of government. We are weak in dramatizing political issues, in party management and in the day-to-day business of politics. All Republicans seem to want to decide party policy but too few want to canvass the voters, man the polls or learn the hard business of campaign management. We seem too often to be all Chiefs and no Indians.

So you see, there is a whale of a lot of room in the Republican party for young men and women who will come in and prepare themselves to take over.

2

The party conflict reaches its climax in the quadrennial national political campaign. The color and pageantry of our political contests from the days of the torchlight parade right down to television contribute some of the most vivid parts of our national folklore. Political campaigns, like war, depend on much more than money, mathematics, and pure reason. They are characterized by faith and often by high feeling, by the music of ritual and tradition, by the public clash of personalities.

The campaign is inaugurated by that unique American institution, the nominating convention. Ever since Andrew

Jackson established the nominating convention it has remained pretty much the same, from the days of the lusty agrarian society in an age of canal boats and oxcarts down to the modern era of aircraft and television.

Many people say that the national convention is an archaic institution. They say conventions are unrepresentative and often boss-ridden. They speak of smoke-filled rooms. They ridicule the lumbering formalism, as well as the bands, parades, and unending oratory. The point is also made that too often strong and able candidates kill each other off because none can achieve a majority. Then, it is said, a few leaders select a compromise candidate who is a weak or colorless figure with the unlovely virtue of having stood for little and made no enemies.

All these criticisms have a certain amount of merit, and, in some respects, each of them is well founded. Some of the speeches can be very dull and I can assure you that some of the freak stunts and street parades can be thoroughly irritating to those who are engaged in the serious business of the convention.

Conventions of all kinds, however, are an integral part of the American scene, whether they are political, American Legion, or Elks. There are hundreds of conventions going on all the time—of jewelers, buttonhole makers, lumbermen, economists, university professors, and farm organizations. The convention is as thoroughly American as corn-on-the-cob and I hope our people never lose their desire to get together with one another to discuss problems, find solutions, and also have a little fun.

The spirited atmosphere of our national political conventions has another important purpose. It is part of the tested process by which the major national parties compete for popular support and popular imagination. No one has invented a more effective way of bringing concentrated attention to political matters of the greatest importance to the country, and of bringing about ultimate agreement on policies and candidates.

Agreement must be reached and perhaps there is no better way than jamming two thousand hot, weary people, who are running short of cash and time, into a jury room as big as a convention city and keeping them there until they make a decision. Behind all the sound and fury lies the massive common sense and accumulated wisdom of our party system.

In the shaping of the party platforms there is much more hard work and useful clash of ideas than ever appears to the casual observer. Weeks in advance of the convention the National Committee selects a tentative chairman of the platform committee who assembles a staff and goes to work. Conferences are held with members of the party from all ranks and with groups from all parts of the country. Platform drafts are ready by the time of the convention. The full platform committee is selected at the beginning of the convention and then the real fights start. The members of the committee work day and night, thrashing out the issues and the way in which party principles should be stated. The controversy often boils over on the floor of the convention, where it is fought out again and settled by votes of the delegates.

The leading candidates for the nomination influence the

33

platform considerably. Sometimes one candidate is in control of the National Committee and is able to dictate the choice of a chairman and the makeup of the platform committee. Then other candidates with differing views must make their opinions felt through the weight of their supporters on the platform committee, and ultimately among the delegates as a whole. I have been in both positions and believe me, the contest can be hard and acrimonious.

It is interesting historically that out of the conflict of views the more liberal position usually prevails. Both platforms on which I ran in 1944 and 1948 were generally good and progressive documents. On the other hand, some provisions of both platforms were so vague on some points, as a result of compromise, as to justify the frequent assertion that the party platform means what the candidate says it means.

3

A good deal of mystery has been made of the manner in which nominations for President are brought about. It is complicated rather than mysterious, and that is just because the parties are complex and so is human nature.

First of all, who are the delegates who make the decision? They are well over a thousand men and women in each party, plus an equal number of alternate delegates. The number of delegates and alternates for each party usually changes every four years; and each party changes the basis for selection from time to time. Delegates and alternates are variously selected by party primaries, party congressional district and state conventions and by party state committees.

I have previously pointed out that each party is really forty-eight [now fifty] separate parties, one in each state. Again, we should note, delegates are picked on a state basis, not on a national basis. The national convention is the crucible where the divergent elements from forty-eight states are fused.

Long before the delegates are selected several names are in the minds of people as possible presidential nominees. Often, announced candidates are traveling around the country, making their views known and meeting the people, including, of course, party leaders and prospective delegates.

Each prospective nominee has friends and supporters in almost every state who have undertaken to support his candidacy. Sometimes unwanted strangers endeavor to attach themselves to the movement and this often creates considerable embarrassment for the candidate. Here the old adage is particularly true, "I can handle my enemies but Heaven protect me from my friends." The hitchhikers who are always climbing aboard every political movement for their own purposes, are the bane of the existence of a presidential candidate.

Much has been said and written suggesting that nominations are secured as a result of unconscionable bargains, private commitments, and actual purchase of delegate support. In my own experience this was not the case. In the three national conventions in which I have been involved,

35

while I may have been fortunate or naïve, I made no private commitments nor was the support of any delegate ever purchased or the promise of a public office ever made to anyone.

Perhaps the most important single influence in the decision of the delegates is whether they believe a candidate can win if he is nominated. Many factors enter into this decision. They usually include a consideration of the candidate's record of success in winning elections in his own state and perhaps in presidential primaries. Of course, delegates like to have a candidate from their own section of the country who understands their own particular problems. Many are influenced by his record as an administrator or by his social and economic views as expressed in legislation he has supported or sponsored.

Frequently delegates are pledged in advance to a given candidate by action of the conventions in their states or by the results of presidential primaries. Others have promised a candidate their votes on the basis of personal friendship or old loyalties. Still others are committed to favorite sons either on the basis of state pride or as a temporary hiding-place until they can see which way the wind is blowing in the convention.

The managers of each candidate arrive in advance of the convention and the delegates are furiously buttonholed and bombarded as they reach the convention city. Sometimes the various managers have collected a list of the friends and associates of many of the delegates and try to get them to influence the delegate to support their candidate. As the party leaders arrive many of them announce their choice of candidates and each announcement has an impact upon convention sentiment.

By the time the convention opens, the claims of the managers of the candidates usually become more realistic unless a particular candidate's position is really desperate. The members of the press have been busy scouting out their estimates of the strength of the various candidates as the delegates were selected at primaries and conventions.

When the balloting starts, every candidate wants to show enough strength to be one of the leaders on the first ballot. He also wants to have enough strength in reserve so he can gain on the psychologically important second ballot. For example, in 1940, I led on the first three ballots out of six—the wrong three. I lost ground on the second ballot. That was the beginning of the end and everybody knew it.

As the balloting progresses, favorite sons withdraw and the switching of votes usually makes a trend clear. Before long there is a rush to the bandwagon of the indicated winner. When it is all over, almost everyone is eagerly establishing party harmony or grimly pretending to do so, to go forward to win the election.

Now, where does the "smoke-filled room" come in? It comes in where there are enough strong candidates to prevent anyone from getting a majority and there is a stalemate. When that happens there are frantic conferences to create a coalition between two leaders, usually with one for President and one for Vice-President. If this effort fails because no two are willing to get together or are able to transfer their support, the stalemate is complete.

Then there are efforts in many smoke-filled rooms to

reach agreement on a compromise candidate. By this time rivalries and tempers have reached a point where the candidate who is finally acceptable to all factions is likely to be one who has evoked neither great enthusiasms nor great enmities. Fortunately, this unhappy process has not occurred too often.

Some have proposed that in order to eliminate all of the defects of national conventions in one fell swoop, the present convention system should be abolished. They propose that party primaries be held in each of the forty-eight states with the results binding upon the delegates. Such a proposal would make the nomination for President nothing but a popularity contest in each state. If one candidate should win a majority of the delegates from all the states, he would be nominated automatically and the convention, like the Electoral College, would merely ratify the results. Otherwise there would be a deadlocked convention made up of delegates instructed for a variety of candidates. Then, presumably the delegates would all be free to shift their votes and the smoke-filled room would really take over.

Worse than this, who could possibly run in ten or twenty primaries, to say nothing of thirty or forty? Nobody could stand the physical strain of such widespread travel and continuous speaking.

Moreover, no candidate could possibly devote himself so exclusively to the pursuit of the presidency unless he were either very wealthy or unemployed. Certainly, no one holding responsible office either in the Congress or as governor of a state could ever again be nominated for President under such a system.

The expense would also be prohibitive. The cost of each candidacy would run into many millions of dollars and if such sums could be raised, which I doubt, their expenditure would create a public revulsion.

Among all the suggested alternatives, it appears to me that the convention system is still the best. It can be and should be improved but despite its defects, no one has yet produced a better method of declaring party policy and selecting nominees. I doubt that they will.

The methods of change in our political system are remarkably effective. Our political system has saved us from all the violent methods employed by absolute monarchies and dictatorships. It has also saved us from the fatal divisions and paralysis which are characteristic of nations plagued by a multiplicity of parties. This alone would provide reason enough for the system.

4

One of the standard weapons of party conflict both between conventions and during campaigns is the effort to pin labels on individuals or movements, attractive or sinister, depending upon the point of view. On the whole, the Democratic party in recent years has been the more successful in this use of semantics.

One of the most intriguing words in the political lexicon is the word "liberal." It is a touchstone eagerly sought by almost every political group. After a long and useful life, it still has warmth and confers a kind of pleasant aura upon those who garb themselves in its benign appeal. The trouble is that the word has been used to describe widely differing views and objectives and it has been sadly corrupted.

The traditional meaning of the word "liberal" described a movement to restrict the power of government over the lives of people. It came into active use in the new age ushered in by the eighteenth century when the Western world was striking off the shackles of royal absolutism. Society was to be governed by new concepts of individual freedom, equality under the law, limited government, and the rule of law instead of the rule of men.

Two hundred years later, the transmutation of the word, as the alchemist would say, has become one of the wonders of our time. Part of the change has come from a broadly based movement to use the powers of government for humanitarian ends.

It is evident that over the last hundred years there has been some loss of control by the individual over his own life. The swift advances of technology, the shift from rural to urban life, the rise of great corporate enterprise and of great unions of labor, the increasing sensitivity and interdependence of our economy—all these have stemmed from the industrial society we have built. While the Industrial Revolution has brought a far higher standard of living for the individual it has also brought him new kinds of insecurity. This, in turn, has bred a collective sense of need for wider control of the forces which everyone now recognizes are far beyond the control of any individual.

After the Western world had achieved freedom from absolutism in government, the Industrial Revolution developed great economic powers in private hands. In the name of liberalism, the power of the state has quite properly been used to limit abuses by the strong and to protect the individual from hazards entirely beyond his control.

While our devotional words politically are still "freedom," "liberty," "independence," "self-reliance," and "individual initiative," many of us find that their meaning has become less clear since the machine came of age. People have looked for a new way to make the old and beloved words fit the new time.

This is the opportunity which the advocates of an all-powerful government have seized. To resolve the dilemma inherent in their desire to claim the name "liberal," they have sought to change its meaning along with the meaning of the word "freedom." According to the neo-liberals, freedom in its classic sense meant only freedom to starve. They say the real meaning is freedom to receive from government all the comforts and security of life. In exchange the individual is expected to do the bidding of government. Both definitions seem a bit extreme.

The higher purpose of the modern collectivists teaches that the legal liberty of the Western world is "formal liberty" without substance and that "actual liberty," as they call it, must be substituted for the traditional freedoms. They say that the old kind of liberty was "license for the few and economic serfdom for the many."

Not only in America, but all over the world, we see men use the word "liberalism" to promote the very policies of

41

government which liberals rose up to destroy. This distortion of the word has led many well-meaning and genuine liberals into a state of confusion. The really disturbing thing about it is that it leads to the unwitting acceptance by an increasing number of people of the instruments of totalitarianism.

In addition to warping the basic concept of liberalism, the corrupters have gone further. I have already indicated that technical advances have prepared people to accept modified concepts of liberty. The supercharged word which powerful, centralized government uses to induce them to go further is "welfare." The centralized government people have taken it over as a latter-day Ark of the Covenant. Moreover, a lot of Republicans have fallen into the abyss by appearing to attack all welfare and that seems to a good many people like firing on the flag.

It must have been some very clumsy Republican—I do not know the origin of the phrase or who perpetrated it—who tried to pin the label "Welfare State" on Mr. Truman's government. Others joined in the clamor and, of course, the Democrats joyously accepted the epithet as a new instrument of party warfare—and party profit.

Of course, they are running a Welfare State. There has never been a responsible government which did not have the welfare of its people at heart. I am proud of the fact that we in the State of New York have made great social welfare advances, as have most of the states.

Anybody who thinks that an attack on the fundamental idea of security and welfare is appealing to people generally, is living in the Middle Ages. Everybody wants welfare and security in one form or another. It makes no difference whether he is a day laborer who wants his social security or a small businessman who wants the value of his savings preserved or the investor who wants the value of his investments preserved. I have never met anybody who did not want welfare and security. The man who first used the phrase "Welfare State" as an epithet against our present government certainly did his cause no good, to put it mildly.

There is no sound or legitimate issue between the parties as to the desirability of security and welfare. The issues—and they are very sharp—lie in the means of achieving agreed objectives without sacrificing other objectives which are equally important.

5

In this changed political environment the role of government today must be redefined. It must be cast in terms of the modern dilemma: How shall we reconcile our fierce tradition of personal freedom with the changes brought by a highly industrialized society?

Is it true that we must accept all-powerful government in the attempt to secure both welfare and liberty? I hope not, because, if it is true, then I think our liberties have lived most of their lives.

A great jurist, a liberal Democrat whom some considered a dangerous radical, the late Justice Louis Brandeis, gave us the answer:

Experience should teach us to be most on our guard to protect liberty when the government's purposes are beneficent. Men born to freedom are naturally alert to repel invasion of their liberty by evil-minded rulers. The greatest dangers to liberty lurk in insidious encroachment by men of zeal, well-meaning but without understanding.

Here, in the words of a great Democrat, is the hard core of the Republican position today. It is the basic issue between the parties. It is not the issue between all Republicans and all Democrats. There are Republicans and Democrats who believe every social advance we have made toward personal security in the last twenty years should be abolished. There are Republicans and Democrats who believe we should rush headlong toward total government security and supervision from the cradle to the grave and some even include nationalization of industry as part of the program.

Disregarding the minority views within the parties, and judging preponderant sentiment by the standards I have previously suggested, the essential difference between the parties lies in the way "to protect liberty when the government's purposes are beneficent." Or, to put it another way, the issue lies in the means of achieving objectives without injury to other objectives.

Some may say that the means are of no importance so long as the objective is achieved. Many people do say it, and it is the sheerest folly. Mussolini made the trains run on time and cleared the streets of beggars. But at what cost?

Hitler offered his people the bait of old-age insurance, full employment, and complete security. In exchange, they gave him their liberties. At the end of the war they found they had no security at all and were living amid scenes of starvation and utter desolation.

Mr. Stalin has similarly provided a kind of minimum drudge security for his people. Soviet old-age insurance, for example, is covered by the simple expedient of seeing that the people work until they drop.

The route you take to achieve objectives is decisive as between freedom and slavery. You can follow the Mussolini, the Hitler, or the Stalin route to security. Hundreds of millions have done so, only to find bitter gall at the end of the rainbow. They found not security but war, slavery, and destruction.

An all-powerful central government can destroy our freedoms more quickly and effectively than can the states or the localities where the people can watch and control what is done. It can move faster but we often pay a terrible price for the speed—and usually its bureaucracy is a stifling failure.

Let me illustrate what I consider a sound route to a social objective. After many years as public prosecutor, both federal and state, I was deeply convinced that government was failing miserably in its duty to attack the problem of juvenile delinquency.

As governor, I asked a special committee of my cabinet to study the problem. After extensive study, they came up with a program. Reduced to simplest terms, it involved an offer by the state to each community of one-half the operating cost of whatever youth services or youth centers it would set up.

The plan was built on a basic principle: our object was to stimulate local community action and to give orders to nobody. It was to capture the imagination of parents, teachers, clergy, and others in each community where the children lived, to do a job themselves according to whatever method they thought was most effective. It was our purpose to encourage people to try their own ideas, to make their own mistakes and learn, but, most of all, to arouse their enthusiastic interest. The plan worked. After five years [in 1950], more than seven hundred youth centers had been set up in the State of New York and juvenile delinquency had dropped some 27 percent.

There was another means of achieving this objective. We could have set up a state agency with five thousand employees instead of the three dozen we now have. Instead of spending the two million dollars the program actually cost, we could easily have spent ten to twenty million dollars a year. That is the way Washington would have done it. That would have cost the people large sums in taxes. That would have concentrated vastly increased political power in Albany. But worst of all, that would have lost to the children of the state the enthusiastic leadership of the people in their own communities.

With our tradition of freedom and our dislike of debts, deficits, oppressive taxes, and great powers in government, why have federal programs made such a successful appeal to our people? I think it is because many millions of Americans have been persuaded that the federal government is the only alternative to necessary depressions and insecurity of life in the machine age. The appeal is based on fear.

But life is more than unemployment, sickness, and old age. Life is alive and vital, to be lived and enjoyed. A morbid government that insists only on acquiring more and more power to spend more and more money from more and more taxes for the negative aspects of life, will end up as all history shows, with no money, no taxes, and no security for its people.

The people were told, and for a long time believed, that the steadily mounting costs of government would not touch them but would fall only upon big business and the rich. But with steadily increasing tax deductions from their paychecks wage earners came to realize that the costs fall on all alike.

The people have been slower to discover that taxes on business are simply a tax on them. For business taxes are merely an additional element of the cost of doing business.

Government has nothing it does not take away from the people. It is an illusion that it alone can deliver security and leisure. In the last analysis, security and leisure, which we all desire, can only be delivered by a vigorous and productive economic system. Under such a system, government can and should promote equal opportunity and a sharing of the good things of life.

If the national government should succeed in acquiring total power in exchange for promises of total security, it will either collapse from within as the Communists prophesy, or it will be overthrown from without by hardier, hairier people who are still prepared to work and achieve.

I believe we must buttress and stimulate reward for achievement. There are only two ways in this world to induce men to create the goods essential to life. One is hunger, compulsion, and the lash. The other is reward. Throughout all our history we have believed in the reward system. It should be strengthened.

The free man wants to increase both human and economic liberty because they are inseparable. The Socialist believes he can preserve human freedom while nationalizing the country's resources. The Communist knows he cannot and he does not want to.

6

I reach four basic conclusions:

First. The advocate of all-powerful, central government denies the great fundamental that the primary purpose of all government is to preserve liberty. By asserting that security is the chief aim of our society, he seeks to turn our people to the lotus and away from the basic truth that without working and producing we perish.

Second. All-powerful, central government requires a special kind of permanent control and continuity and therefore inevitably moves in the direction of the one-party system. It seeks to collect and pay out such a large share of the people's income that any interruption of its multifarious activities would produce hardship and crisis. To carry out this purpose will require the transfer of the power of the public purse from the Congress to the Executive.

Third. All-powerful, central government, like dictatorships, can continue only by growing larger and larger. It can never retrench without admitting failure. It feeds on the gradual obliteration of state and local governments as elements of sovereignty and tends to transform them into districts and prefectures. By absorbing more than half of all the taxing power of the nation, the federal government now deprives the states and local governments of the capacity to support the programs they should conduct. In place of their own taxing powers, it offers them in exchange the counterfeit currency of federal subsidy.

Fourth. All-powerful, central government gradually destroys the mainspring of our society. It offers no incentives to those who must create the goods and services which provide the security. In the words of the ancient writer, it sings a siren song: "Cast in thy lot among us; let us have one purse." It levels all down and throttles the source of our strength which lies in the restless ambitions of the millions of centers of initiative in our individual businesses and on our farms.

In its debut in this country such government has enjoyed considerable success. That is because it has been living on past accumulations of capital and techniques in a period of prosperity growing out of the postwar, worldwide demand for everything America can produce.

It is a fair weather system. One of two perils will catch up with it.

The first peril is in the high taxes, oppressive regulations, delays and frustrations due to massive bureaucracies, inflation of prices and the ominous threat to adequate pro-

49

duction. Each of these factors has an obviously destructive effect. Price inflation is especially virulent because it nullifies the value of the security programs which government uses to justify its existence. It also falls hardest on those in the middle income range—the white collar groups—the people with moderate, fixed incomes, such as teachers, scholars, clergy, and engineers. No free society has ever survived without a successful middle group.

The other peril that will catch up with this kind of government is that, like all governments, it will make mistakes. Whenever a government has become so powerful that the correctives provided by the party system are no longer at hand, you may be sure that the government's mistakes will destroy the nation. To this truth the people of Germany, Italy, and Japan bear eloquent and tragic witness.

7

Human freedom demands that we develop a better method than that of an all-powerful central government.

First of all, we must begin by agreeing among ourselves what the goal of our society should be. I propose that our goal should be the same today as it has been for 175 years: to foster individual liberty as the only means to a society of opportunity and abundance.

For government to act against the insecurities of life in our modern society is not at all inconsistent with a system based on individual competition and reward for everything above minimum security levels. We can build a floor under the uncertainties of life in our industrial economy without putting a ceiling on the height of our building.

Our time is faced with the problems of unemployment, old age, medical care, housing, discrimination, and agricultural price stabilization. Each of these problems can and will be met. But the road to Washington is not the only road.

We can believe in traffic control without agreeing that all traffic regulations should be promulgated from Washington.

We can practice our religion without agreeing that the federal government should appoint and pay the clergy.

We can approve of marriage without having all marriage licenses issued by the Department of Justice.

We must have a tougher and wiser view of the modern dilemma than we have been offered. I propose that we set up criteria by which to judge government action as we seek to reconcile the deep-rooted individualism of our country with the problems of the machine age.

Does the particular welfare measure of government build up the independence and responsibility of the individual citizen or does it make him dependent and subservient?

Does a particular intervention by government widen or narrow the bounds of personal liberty?

Does the proposal deprive any group or segment of our people of any legitimate individual freedom of action they now enjoy?

Does it do by governmental action what people can and should do for themselves by voluntary action?

Does it remove from productive work a substantial number of people in order to administer the program?

Does it have a sound fiscal basis?

Not all of these criteria may be relevant in each case. But they all stand as signposts of the right road.

The central problem of twentieth-century politics remains unsolved. No nation, no system of government has yet succeeded in reconciling the age-old conflict between liberty and authority.

It is our great responsibility, as a people, to press for the solution of that conflict within the framework of our free system.

III

Domestic and Foreign Policy Making under the Two-Party System*

The approaches of the two major American political parties to the solution of domestic and foreign problems are the basis for their claims to the support of the voters. From decade to decade and even from year to year the majority viewpoints within the parties change. This is entirely natural. As I indicated earlier, neither party is really a party at all, but is the sum total of forty-eight [now fifty] different parties in the states, containing the whole panorama of American opinion in all its varying shades.

From time to time various groups within a party combine to give it alternately a conservative, a liberal, an agrarian, or a labor dominance.

Emphasis, also, shifts immediately when a party comes into power. There have been times in the past when the trend of the Republican party, in control nationally, was to increase the power of the central government, just as the

---

* Lectures III and IV of the original series have been combined and extensive discussion of contemporary national legislative problems has been omitted. J.A.W.

53

present [Democratic] administration is endeavoring to do.

Also, subject to exceptions, it is usually the party in power, Republican or Democratic, which has a more internationalist outlook than the party out of power. The Constitution charges the President with responsibility for foreign policy. Responsibility, regardless of party, begets information and necessitates active leadership.

1

Although there is some tendency for the parties to follow similar lines in domestic policy when they are in power, a basic distinction between the parties has evolved. Over the last thirty or forty years this fundamental difference has become fairly clear.

Today, the Democratic party is committed to the steady enlargement of the powers of the federal government. In the 1930s it still gave lip service to local initiative, balanced budgets, and individual enterprise. Today, it gives little support for any of these traditional aspects of our society.

During this transformation of the Democratic party the Republican position has also been modified by events. I doubt if the most conservative Republican would suggest abandonment of such concepts as unemployment insurance, collective bargaining, bank deposit insurance, regulation of security exchanges, or old-age and survivors insurance. Both parties have had a share in advancing these causes.

There are, however, sharp differences between the parties in approach and in the basic philosophy underlying the handling of many existing and future programs.

The leadership of the Democratic party believes almost all problems can be solved by governmental rather than by voluntary action and specifically by the federal government through federal funds, federal personnel, and federal controls.

The Republican approach is first to seek to handle the problem locally and voluntarily by community action, and by public opinion. When these are inadequate, then the solution is first to be attempted by local government, secondly by state and lastly by federal action.

Naturally, I prefer the Republican approach. It utilizes to the full the powerful forces of voluntary effort and local initiative. It employs the energies of existing services, public and private, rather than bypassing or dominating them. This approach would rely on federal action primarily to supply skills or uniformity where these are necessary. It would leave the people free to solve problems as free men rather than as controlled or directed servants of government.

Moreover, this approach leaves the federal government uncluttered with the vast detail of minor services. It should be free to devote its very best talents to the immense problems of world affairs, national defense, national fiscal management, national economic problems, agricultural stability and the broad social action which can only be handled by federal action.

In my view, we should seek policies which solve problems without sacrificing individual liberty or local government. Above all, the line of action should preserve the magic productivity of our free economic system upon which our very existence as a nation depends.

This system has increased the real income of our people by 500 percent in one century. Today, with only seven percent of the world's population, we possess more than half of the world's manufacturing capacity. This enormous achievement has never been equalled under any all-powerful, central government. It will be destroyed if we acquire one.

How shall we preserve what we have, continue to meet our obligations as an active, socially conscious community, avoid the catastrophe of an all-powerful, central government and save individual freedom? Only the outlines of the answers to these questions can be indicated here.

There are many and varied domestic problems facing the national government. They change from time to time particularly as emphasis shifts from social to agricultural to business, labor, racial, or religious discrimination and other areas which emerge as pre-eminent periodically. These compelling demands can be met as need arises, so long as the capacity of the economy can support the demands made upon it. To achieve and maintain this basic strength, I believe there are two domestic responsibilities of the national government which tower far above all others.

First. In its necessary and proper action to influence and maintain business and employment, the federal government should rely on general and not direct controls. By this I mean it should influence the economy mainly through sound monetary and fiscal policies. It should not set up an endless series of direct controls over prices, wages, costs, investments and the like. Direct control puts an army of government employees over private citizens in the conduct of their personal affairs. Direct controls promise to obtain results which are in fact never achieved. The real objective should be to foster the general economic climate in which a free society prospers rather than to adopt the gadgetry of totalitarianism.

Second. The government cannot wisely or effectively control interest rates, or monetary and fiscal policies in aid of the general economy, if it does not first control itself. This means that the second imperative is that it maintain a stable currency by pursuing sound budget policies. History is strewn with the wreckage of nations which failed to keep a sound currency.

Today our government is badly overcommitted financially and it now appears that we will have yet another huge federal deficit. In a time of great business activity, our government is heavily increasing rather than decreasing its huge dollar debt. Nations, like individual families, can get along for a while on borrowed money. But the day of reckoning always comes. Family bankruptcy is an individual tragedy. A national bankruptcy can carry down with it an entire civilization.

2

Important as our domestic problems always are, our foreign affairs today are more critical and are in much deeper disarray. Yet foreign policy is the field which the party out of power and the Congress tend to leave to the President. I believe this is a serious error.

This country faces a crisis today in the conduct of its foreign affairs. The situation is so grave as to require us to concentrate our whole effort as a nation toward its solution. It demands a supreme and unified effort commanding the best experience and brains in the country.

I am profoundly convinced that American initiative can save our freedom and that of much of the world. But the hour is very late.

I do not propose in this lecture to invent a new foreign policy for the United States. Foreign policy is a continuing, developing thing. I do propose that as a nation we think clearly and act decisively in ten major respects and that we do so forthwith.

3

The first necessity is to reverse the ominously rising trend toward isolationism in the United States. While paying lip service to international responsibility, there is a drift in the

United States toward withdrawing governmentally from international cooperation and collective security.

Such a movement can come only from ignorance of the catastrophic effects upon our way of life which will inevitably follow continued Communist successes. It should not be necessary to continue reminding our people and the leaders of public opinion that as a nation we have twice concluded that the freedom of Western Europe is a condition of our own security. Regardless of the immediate causes, the fundamental is that we have gone to war twice in this century because danger to the freedom of Europe endangered us. Now, with the world so shrunken, this should be much clearer than ever before.

It is a plain fact that if we should make the fatal error of choosing an isolationist course, we would then simply be following the advice of every agent of the Kremlin. We would actually be collaborating with the Soviet. All we need do to serve the Communist purpose is to withdraw within our borders and abandon the rest of the world for them to conquer. Then, we would soon be really isolated. We would be surrounded and encircled. It would then be no task at all for a Communist world to strangle us to death without ever bothering to drop a bomb.

The repercussions of our isolation and encirclement would be cumulative and endless. The loss of foreign markets would produce drastic consequences. The loss of the raw materials we receive from overseas would impose such staggering costs in the development of substitutes and synthetics for the essentials of our modern industrial life that

59

the living standards of our people would steadily decline, while government regimentation would take us into a complete economic autarchy.

On top of that, the cost of maintaining armaments adequate to defend our 150,000,000 people [195,000,000 in 1966] against the possible attacks of two billion people would alone force us to sacrifice our free way of life.

With one third of the world already conquered, if another third should go, even the most die-hard isolationists on the one extreme and the soft-headed left-wingers on the other, would realize that America could not survive alone in a Communist world.

We can, of course, just sit and wait for this to happen. Then all America would be at last aroused to its peril. Then, also, it would be too late.

4

The "happy thought" approach to foreign policy is typified in the area of elegant nonsense, by a publicity stunt of a group which spent a widely advertised $167, trying to get President Truman on the telephone, speaking in English, to Premier Stalin, speaking in Russian. There were also proposals by a former U. S. Senator and a former Vice-President of the United States to buy peace from Russia by offering to pay her many billions of dollars. The tragedy is that many people are willing to accept such nonsense as constructive. We will not get peace through gimmicks. We cannot buy it by either ransom or tribute. It is a cruel delusion to lead people to believe it can be done.

Another in the series of "happy thought" solutions comes from those who believe that all would be well if only we would break off diplomatic relations with the Soviet Union and its satellites. Their argument is that continuing diplomatic relations with them implies their respectability and, moreover, that it provides a one-way street for Soviet spies. The latter may be true, but should we save the Russians the trouble of erecting an iron curtain? Breaking off diplomatic relations would compel us to depend on third parties for all our communication with Communist countries. Worst of all, it would seem to many worried people throughout the world that we were depriving ourselves of all chance of working directly for peace and that we were slamming the door against peaceful solutions.

Then there is the idea that all could be solved if the Big Three could just have a talk. That is a lovely idea, but I am afraid history will not deal too kindly with the occasions when Presidents of the United States have sat down to have a talk with the heads of other nations whether at Versailles, Teheran, Yalta, or Potsdam. Moreover, if we have a Big Three, then we affront France because the Conference is not a Big Four.

Even if such a conference were to be held after the most exhaustive exploration and careful preparation, there is no assurance it would be successful. Meanwhile, high hopes would rise in the breasts of people everywhere and mankind would wait breathlessly for every word from the meeting. If definitive solutions were not reached, a sense of disillusionment would follow and even a sense of doom. It would be taken as a sign that, all other methods having been exhausted, war was inevitable.

Sometimes it is as important to avoid doing bad things as it is to do good things. Historically, we have been most successful in foreign affairs when we have conducted them through customary channels by trained diplomats.

The belief that any single "happy thought" solution would bring an end to the cold war and peace to the world should be avoided like the plague.

Surely, no suggestion should be overlooked and no possibility omitted from study and possible action. But there is no substitute for the hard labor of experts with a lifetime of training, working patiently and with devotion in the cause of peace. There is no substitute for strength, competence, patience, and determination.

5

Even as we reject diplomatic panaceas, we should also reject the notion that war is inevitable. Fatalistic acceptance of the inevitability of war is the one thing most likely to bring it on.

Wars usually occur when one nation believes it can win a quick and easy victory, as Germany hoped to do in each of the last three wars she started. War is not normally launched against a powerful nation ready to defend itself. If the United States has a strong defense establishment, war will be less likely. Of course, no prudent man can believe that war is impossible but, in the same way, no wise man would propose it or assert its inevitability.

Our purpose must be to make it clear to any aggressor that there can be no limited risks in a war against the free world; that the risks of atomic warfare are total and that, regardless of what damage might be done to us, instant and terrible retaliation would be exacted.

Obviously, war might occur if the members of the Politburo should face such serious internal difficulties that they believe war is the only means of keeping themselves in power. For the moment, they are justified in assuming that they are winning the world without war. If their conquests should be stopped, they would still have large enough areas to consolidate to keep them busy for a long time.

Those who believe in the inevitability of war should remember that the entire Soviet program is based upon the conviction that American economic and political collapse must come. When it does not come, they will be required to reorient their entire program, always provided we have been successful in the meantime in preventing them from taking the rest of the world.

We are buying time with our billions of dollars for foreign aid and our billions for defense. If we are faithful to our commitments and to the cause in which we believe, we have a right to hope that time is on our side.

6

To win the cold war, we must put our whole strategy on a new basis. It is not enough to speak of diplomacy. There must be corresponding counsel and action. Among other things, we urgently need to know what is going on in the world far better than we know it today. To be blunt, I believe our intelligence system is wholly inadequate for a country facing the dangers and responsibilities before us.

I was appalled to see the dissipation of our intelligence contacts and sources following the end of the Second World War. This was just part and parcel of the administration's light-hearted and unrealistic attitude of the postwar days toward our relations with Russia.

We have made a fair start with a new Central Intelligence Agency on the long and painful job of rebuilding. But our structure of defense has at least in part been based on grave miscalculations. We have, at times, been living in a fool's paradise based on misinformation and misinterpretations of the information we had. The safety of the whole cause of freedom depends upon the best intelligence work possible.*

* Obviously the CIA has now developed greatly in skill and depth, as Governor Dewey so earnestly hoped, sixteen years ago. The intelligence gap that was so dangerous at that time may well have been closed.   J.A.W.

7

Hand in hand with a good intelligence service goes an effective information service. Our information efforts should be enormously intensified in an effort to reach the peoples of Russia and her satellite subjects and the neutral or unconvinced peoples of the world.

The Communist Empire is peculiarly sensitive to the truth—to facts. This vulnerability is evidenced by the fantastic precautions the Communist governments take to deny or limit foreign contacts with their people.

In the essential broadening of our information and persuasive efforts we should use all our resources. Among others, right here in the United States and elsewhere in the free world, we have representative leaders of the governments of satellite states that once were free. They come from practically all non-Communist groups in these countries. We should get their message of hope to the peoples of their countries.

I am glad to see that a start is being made by the National Committee for Free Europe through Radio Free Europe to put the message of these men on the air. It is late but not too late to mobilize their genius and talents. They can be effectively used in the world struggle for the minds and hearts of people. There is talent here available for the asking, accompanied by passionate devotion to our common cause.

8

Intelligence and propaganda are, of course, merely tools. They must be directed to great ends. As a nation, we must decide what it is we want and then pursue it by every course and means available.

During the First World War we said we wanted nothing for ourselves and nothing is what we got.

In the Second World War again we said we wanted nothing and again nothing is what we got.

At other times in our history we have known what we wanted and got it. Consider the War of 1812. The actual hostilities were indecisive and often humiliating for us. But at the peace conference which produced the Treaty of Ghent, the United States won a very advantageous frontier with Canada and all the other national objects for which we had fought. That was a war we did not win but we won the peace.

During this last war, it was Russia who knew exactly what she wanted. The Soviet was represented by able, ruthless men who usually got exactly what they wanted or a large portion of it, including 100,000,000 subjects in Central Europe, an advantageous split of Austria, a similar split of Germany, an isolated Berlin, an agreement to extract huge reparations from Italy, and wholesale spoliation in Germany, Austria, and Manchuria. She also acquired a third of Korea as well as a dominant position in Port Arthur, Dairen, the Chinese Eastern and South Manchuria Railroads and other objectives.

As for our wanting nothing, or to put it another way, not knowing what we did want, we have again got nothing but a bad peace and a shrinking free world. It is time for us to know what we want and to go after it.

Our objectives need not, indeed they should not, be selfish or material. But they must be real, they must be clearly defined and universally understood, at least by our own representatives. They must serve not only our own security but the cause of a free world.

I cannot make it too plain that if we do not substantially determine the course of events, then events will be determined by others at our expense.

In addition to overwhelming force for peace we must add a genuine and united understanding of what we really want in world affairs this year, next year and for generations to come.

9

One basic objective should be a United States of Europe. For some unaccountable reason, both this nation and the nations of Europe have backed into this entire subject with an appalling lethargy.

The 270,000,000 people of free Europe are nearly twice as many as we have in the United States. Many European countries have long traditions of self-government and important colonial associations overseas. If they remain separated by tariffs and national rivalries, with trade impeded by unstable currencies, the future of Europe is dark. But with economic unity, stable currency, and joint military defense, Europe could also achieve political unity and be a most powerful force in the world for peace, freedom, and stability.

A provision was inserted into the first Marshall Plan bill, which stated that European cooperation was one of the objectives of the Plan. Despite this provision of the Plan very little unity has been achieved.

I am aware of all of the difficulties. But many of the ablest and most responsible leaders of European countries have expressed strong support for a united Europe. Almost everybody is for the idea, but progress has been far too slow. A united Europe could be a cornerstone of a free world.

10

The next imperative among our foreign policy objectives is that we stop regarding the continuous Red successes in Asia with the calm of a Buddha contemplating his navel.

The fantastic reversals of America's official attitude concerning the Far East and particularly China, during the last five years [from 1945 to 1950], would have been ludicrous if they were not so tragic. In 1945 the Nationalist government, headed by Chiang Kai-shek, was our beloved ally which had been nobly resisting Japanese aggression for fifteen years. The sacrifices of the Chinese people were legendary and heartrending and their leaders were received in this country with almost reverential acclaim.

It was in that very year, 1945, at Yalta, that Chinese property and rights were bargained away to Russia. It was in December of that same year that President Truman announced that he was sending Secretary George C. Marshall to China, under an impossible directive to compel the Chinese government to accept a merger with the Communist leaders or face the loss of American aid. It was during that period that we began reading articles in respectable American magazines that the Chinese Communists were really not Communists at all but just charming agrarian reformers.

In November of 1947 I endeavored to call the attention of the nation to what I saw as an impending tragedy of world-shaking consequences. Warning that a continuation of our policy, or absence of policy, would result in the Communist conquest of 450,000,000 traditional friends and allies of America, I pleaded for a reversal of our national policies while aid could still be effective. Others made the same appeal and even as late as midsummer of 1949, when nearly half of China was still under the control of the Nationalist government, I made one final plea, but without avail.

There is no sense now in endeavoring to assess which of two Presidents or five Secretaries of State or what other individuals or factors were responsible. The simple fact is that from Yalta on we never made a real try to help those who had stood with us in our darkest hour.

I am acutely aware of all of the criticisms of the Na-

tionalist government of China but I can never forget that
it was good enough for us during the four years of war
when we needed it and it remained our friend as the new
struggle developed. Yet from Yalta on we treated the Chinese leaders in a fashion which precisely suited the purpose
of their conquering Communist enemies.

Is all lost in the Far East? I hope not. Free governments
still exist in South Korea, Japan, and important areas in
Southeast Asia. The Pacific must not become a Communist lake. The safety of America cries out for a constructive
policy and creative action in the Far East. It is of the first
importance that whatever action we take serves to encourage a restoration of the faith of the peoples of Asia in
America or at least in their own freedom and independence.

11

If our efforts for peace are to succeed, we must do still
more. We must revitalize the Western tradition of developing the underdeveloped areas of Asia and Africa.

For more than four hundred years this course was pur-
sued primarily for individual or national profit, often at the
expense and exploitation of native peoples. The general
approach was condescending; it was "the white man's
burden." Great advances were made in productivity, in
combating disease, in education. But the techniques and
atmosphere in which these gains were made are now out-
dated. The very advances of the native peoples which re-
sulted, brought about a steadily rising desire for freedom

and self-government which it is our policy and our duty to encourage.

Following the example we set in Cuba and in the Philippines, the age of European colonial empires is waning in Asia, as it did in this hemisphere. In Africa the same process is going on. The only expanding, exploiting, imperialistic empires today are Communist.

It is essential that the withdrawal of Western dominance in favor of native governments should not be a prelude to the establishment of a new and vastly worse Communist tyranny and exploitation.

American technical and industrial skill can create great strength and friendships in underdeveloped areas. American investments, with reasonable guarantees by both the American and native governments, seem essential to the continuing progress of the development of the world. They are equally vital to the supply of things we regard as necessities in our own economy and to the world-wide exchange of goods which is an essential characteristic of a free world.

12

The greatest need of our foreign policy is its immediate and sincere restoration to a genuine bi-partisan basis. The two-party system has served us well in dealing with domestic problems. It can also be made to serve the dire necessities of our situation in the world. If this is to be achieved, it requires a radical improvement in the attitude of both the Democratic national administration and sections of the Republican party.

I am not prepared to assert that, in a normal, peaceful world, foreign policy should always be bi-partisan. But it seems to me crystal clear that when the very existence of our country is under continuous and successful attack, it is imperative that foreign policy be bi-partisan or, as Senator Arthur H. Vandenberg used to call it, "un-partisan."

The world situation calls for largeness of spirit in our national leadership. It requires that within our two-party system the leaders must be willing to work together when the nation is exposed to external perils even though they disagree and may contest vigorously on domestic issues.

At best bi-partisan foreign policy is not easily achieved. Clearly, a better and firmer system of cooperation can and must be devised and firmly established at least for the duration of the cold war. Bi-partisan foreign policy is not achieved by the President appointing a few members of the party out of power to his cabinet or to ambassadorships or to other positions of high responsibility in his administration. As soon as a person accepts such an appointment, he is a member of the administration and owes his loyalty to the President.

Consultation must take place before, not after, decisions in the shaping of policy are made. All relevant information must be made available by the administration to the proper representatives of the minority party. Bi-partisanship cannot be merely a ratification of policies determined by the party in power and it should apply in all decisive areas of foreign policy, not merely in those where it is found convenient or politically expedient by that party.

Bi-partisan cooperation also implies, in the nation's welfare, freedom fairly to criticize and to improve legislation on foreign policy matters. It must not mean that the Congress or the leaders of the party out of power are reduced to the status of rubber stamps. It requires a willingness on both sides to work together for great objectives and to rise above personal prejudices and irritations which inevitably flow from differences on domestic policy. To save the peace through our own efforts and with others in the United Nations requires our finest abilities and our highest patriotism.

To any sincere offer of bi-partisanship in a time of crisis, the Republican party must, of course, respond. During ten critical years and as the Republican candidate for President in two national campaigns I made every effort to achieve genuine bi-partisanship; in some areas this was successful, in others the rebuffs were discouraging. Where and when bi-partisanship was competently and sincerely practiced—as in the European Recovery Program—there was unity, strength, and a stunning measure of success.

Where the administration has put partisan concern first, there has been disunity, weakness, and failure. This, in turn, has led to a resurgence of isolationism and opened the door to attacks upon the personnel and policies of the Department of State. But before any Republican rejoices at the possible shipwreck of the foreign policy of the Democratic administration, he should remember that all of us Americans are in the same boat.

73

To sum up: As we make progress in the ten areas of action I have discussed, we should avoid one great danger: the danger that our people will acquire a sense of frustration from the present stalemate and move toward a mood of appeasement. Then we must be on our guard lest we fall prey to one of the strategic retreats which Lenin and Stalin have described as part of the Communist technique. We could easily be trapped into what appeared to be a satisfactory settlement, while Communist forces move stealthily forward.

Or our greatest danger may come when the Soviet and Chinese leaders of the moment consent to smile, to grant friendly interviews to roving journalists and politicians, and assure the world that all is well and that we should relax. If we ever do relax and abandon our weapons, our fate is already written in the history of Czechoslovakia, Poland, Hungary, and a dozen other countries.

Some of the action I have called for has been or is being taken in whole or in part. But the total impact is inadequate both at home and abroad. A major reason for this is that domestic policies dominate the scene and our national capital conveys the impression of fiddling while freedom burns.

The tone of our political affairs can only be set by the President himself. If politics is the theme of the Executive Branch of the government in a time of world crisis, it is difficult to rebuke the Congress for irresponsible votes in dealing with foreign affairs. If the survival of the American republic in the midst of a perilous cold war be accepted by the Chief Executive as our major national purpose, then I

74

am sure his efforts will receive unstinted support and co-operation from the vast majority of the American people and from both political parties. Our political system can indeed be made to work as well in the winning of the cold war as it did in the winning of the Second World War. It can lead a troubled world through its period of greatest peril.

Freedom is never won. It is only preserved from day to day by everlasting vigilance.

Appendix

THOMAS EDMUND DEWEY was born in Owosso, Michigan, on March 24, 1902, the son of George Martin Dewey, Jr., publisher of the Owosso *Times*, and the grandson of its founder. His father was also an active political leader, and his grandfather was one of the delegates to the first Republican state convention held under the oaks in Jackson, Michigan, in 1854.

Governor Dewey was educated in the Owosso public schools, and at the University of Michigan. Upon graduation from the university, he went East to New York and entered Columbia Law School. There he received his LLB in 1925 and became an associate in a prominent New York law firm.

In this same year the young lawyer also became active in the Republican organization in the 10th Assembly District and was soon appointed an election district captain. He also joined the New York Young Republican Club, in which he made steadfast friends who were to become key associates throughout his future career. Four years after joining the club, he was elected Chairman of the Board of Governors.

On June 16, 1928, he married Frances Eileen Hutt, a promising young mezzo-soprano. Today they have two sons in their thirties, Thomas E. Dewey, Jr. and John M. Dewey, and one grandson.

The year 1931 marked a major turning point in Thomas Dewey's young career. Eight days before his twenty-ninth birthday, he was appointed Chief Assistant United States Attorney for the Southern District of New York. While the appointment meant a substantial reduction in salary, it offered the challenge of administering the work of an office of sixty lawyers. It also offered a rare opportunity to gain extensive experience in the trial of important cases and to participate at the heart of the embryonic struggle against organized crime. There he compiled a record as an administrator and as a hardhitting, winning prosecutor. At that time he did not have the remotest interest in a political career and so, as soon as his three years were up, he returned to what would always be his preferred occupation—the private practice of law. He did continue thereafter to serve as a Special Assistant Attorney General of the United States in an important tax case, as well as acting as unpaid special counsel to the City Bar Association in the removal of a Municipal Court judge.

By the summer of 1935, organized crime in New York City had wormed its way into the very heart of the city's political and economic life. Its influence had permeated political ranks at all levels and even the judiciary. The situation had deteriorated to the extent that complaints had a way of finding their way back to the implicated gangsters, and apathy was the accepted official posture. Finally, after months of frustration, a New York Grand Jury rose up in anger and declared open war. It demanded that Governor Herbert H. Lehman bypass the District Attorney and appoint a special prosecutor in charge of an investigation of organized crime in New York County. From his record as a federal prosecutor, the obvious choice for the job was Thomas E. Dewey, and under his direction the office attained complete autonomy, with special police, investigators, and attorneys functioning outside all political domain. Some of the more conspicuous achievements of the racket prosecution were the successful apprehension and prosecution of: a city-wide ring of loan sharks; the Dutch Schultz mob of restaurant racketeers; Arthur "Toots" Herbert, labor leader and king of the poultry racket; Louis "Lepke" Buchalter, head of the gangsters who terrorized the baking and garment industries; Charles "Lucky" Luciano and the other czars of organized crime, as well as a large number of lesser luminaries who ruled the trucking, farm produce, and construction rackets.

In the light of such achievements, it was not surprising that Dewey was drafted in 1937 to run for District Attorney of New York County on the fusion ticket with Mayor Fiorello H. La Guardia. Running as the candidate of city fusion forces, he defeated his opponent by a resounding majority.

As District Attorney, some of Dewey's major achievements were: his successful prosecution of James J. Hines, a leading boss of Tammany Hall (convicted of using political influence to protect criminals); exposure of the criminals in the political organization of Albert Marinelli, the Democratic New York County Clerk who was driven from office; exposure of corruption on the part of Martin Manton, Senior Judge of the U.S. Court of Appeals; and convictions of Fritz Kuhn, the leader of the Nazi bund, as a common thief and Clarence A. Hathaway, editor of the Communist *Daily Worker*, for criminal libel.

A year later, Governor Lehman, one of the greatest vote-getters in the history of the state, announced his decision to retire from the Albany scene and run for the U.S. Senate. The Republicans nominated Thomas E. Dewey for governor, and the Democrats pressured Lehman into giving up his Senatorial aspirations and running again for governor.

Dewey privately conceded his chances against Lehman were faint, but he waged an aggressive campaign—and the outcome was electrifyingly close; he lost by only 1.4 percent of the votes cast. In the same election, the Republican candidate for Senator was defeated by more than 400,000 votes.

Dewey lost, but as a result of the campaign the Republican party gained control of both houses of the legislature, and Thomas E. Dewey emerged as the strongest Republican in the state and one of the leading Republicans in the nation.

In 1939, the Republican party had a dearth of possible candidates to run against President Roosevelt, who was then riding the crest of his New Deal popularity. The Republicans had failed miserably at the polls in 1932 and 1936. In 1938, when Dewey was nosed out by Governor Lehman, Robert A. Taft was elected to the U.S. Senate for the first time, and Wendell L. Willkie was still known as a Democrat.

In the fall of 1939 the thirty-seven-year-old District Attorney and Republicans throughout the country were stunned by public opinion polls which showed Dewey with a towering lead over all other possible candidates for the Republican nomination for President. Republican leaders came to New York in increasing numbers to urge him to run for the nomination and, in December 1939, he agreed. He waged a vigorous campaign, speaking throughout the United States, and entered a number of primaries, all of which he won. Meanwhile Senator Taft and Wendell Willkie were mounting equally vigorous campaigns for the nomination, with Willkie gaining rapidly as the Republican National Convention of June 1940 approached. While Dewey led on the first three ballots, Willkie won the nomination on the sixth, losing the election in the fall to President Roosevelt.

After the convention, Dewey returned to his duties in the District Attorney's office and in the fall campaigned vigorously for Willkie. In the following year, with his four-year term as District Attorney coming to an end, Dewey determined to return again to the private practice of law. In June of 1941 he announced that he would not run for a second term and called on all parties to agree on an outstanding man to carry the torch of a non-political, aggressive District Attorney's office. He proposed the names of four of his assistants, and astute Democratic leadership seized quickly upon one, Frank S. Hogan, a Democrat. The other parties agreed unanimously, after Dewey gave his assurance that he would back Hogan against any other nominee. For the past twenty-five years Frank Hogan has carried on with the support of all parties, conducting the finest office of its kind in the nation.

The spring of 1941 also brought World War II ominously nearer to America. There were millions of our young men under arms in hastily constructed camps all over the country. They suffered many hardships, one of which was the complete lack of facilities for any off-duty relaxation. To meet this need the six service organizations founded the USO. Its first requirement was for a chairman to direct its nation-wide drive for funds. Thomas E. Dewey undertook the task. In that summer he organized a nation-wide campaign with a goal of $10,600,000. At the end of the campaign, more than $16,000,-000 had been contributed.

Dewey returned to private practice once again, but not for long. In 1942, the New York Republicans again nominated him for governor, and this time he won—by almost 650,000 votes. He was to be returned to this office twice more, by similar margins, to become the first governor in the history of the state to win three consecutive four-year terms.

As Governor of New York State, Thomas E. Dewey naturally became a leading candidate for the Republican nomination for President in 1944. He did not seek the nomination, and made no speeches outside of New York State during the pre-convention period. The national Republican leaders who had been his supporters in 1940, and many others, pressed his cause. When Willkie withdrew from the race after his defeat in the Wisconsin primary, Dewey's unanimous nomination on the first ballot at the national convention was virtually assured.

The 1944 presidential campaign was fought under the shadows cast by America's life and death commitment to winning the Second World War. Faithful to his belief in bi-partisanship in times of national emergency, Governor Dewey conducted a deliberately restrained campaign and repeatedly refused to do or say anything which might shake the nation's capacity to win the war. Many assert that had it not been for Dewey's determination to respect this ideal, the outcome could very well have been reversed. Still, it was an astonishingly close election, with Roosevelt winning by a majority of 53.8 percent.

In 1946, Dewey was re-elected governor with an impressive majority, and again became a leading possibility for the Republican nomination for President in 1948. However, Senator Robert A. Taft and former Governor Harold E. Stassen were announced and determined candidates for the nomination. Dewey, during the Oregon primary, soundly defeated Stassen in the first nation-wide radio debate. He went on to defeat Taft and Stassen for the nomination at the national convention in Philadelphia.

The story of the 1948 upset is political history. The pollsters thought the result was certain and stopped their work by October 15. The Republicans were overconfident. Truman effectively attacked the record of the Eightieth Congress, elected in 1946, the first Congress controlled by the Republicans for many years. Whatever the reason, Truman won, although his popular vote totaled less than 50 percent of the votes.

In 1952, the year his best-selling book, *Journey to the Far Pacific*,* was published, Thomas E. Dewey was in the middle of his third term as Governor of New York and determined to return once and for all to private practice as soon as the term was up. He had announced that under no circumstances would he again become a candidate for President, and he had already been the first leading Republican to support the candidacy of Dwight D. Eisenhower.

His support was far more than verbal. Mobilizing his powerful moderate-liberal friends within the party, Governor Dewey took a leading part in securing delegates for Eisenhower, and he provided tough, efficient, but self-effacing leadership for the general. Without this support, it is doubtful that Eisenhower could have won the nomination over Taft.

During his unprecedented twelve years as Governor of New York, Thomas E. Dewey's administration achieved remarkable advances for the people of New York. To list but a few: State aid to education was increased 200 percent, and a tremendous expansion of higher education facilities was initiated, including the creation of a State University with its twenty-seven affiliated colleges and numerous locally operated community colleges. Vast health programs were implemented, and expenditures on mental hygiene were tripled. The Dewey housing program doubled the slum clearance and public housing loan funds and increased annual subsidies fivefold. An intensive highway program was launched, and the governor personally led a bitter fight to win approval of a farm-to-market road net-

* Doubleday & Company, Inc., 1952.

work and the self-supporting cross-state expressway which the legislature in 1964 named, in tribute to him, The Governor Thomas E. Dewey Thruway. Under the governor's leadership, New York State became the first state in the nation to forbid by law racial or religious discrimination in employment, public housing, and education; the Department of Commerce was created and state encouragement to industry became a fact. Also initiated was a broad sickness and disability program, while unemployment insurance and workmen's compensation benefits were expanded and modernized. And all these progressive innovations were accomplished within a conservative balanced budget—and tax rates that were 10 percent below those in force in 1941.

In 1954, despite public and private urging and the appeals of his party, Governor Dewey remained steadfast in his resolve not to run for a fourth term. Since then he has repeatedly declined all inducements to re-enter public service in either an elective or an appointive capacity. He is engaged in private practice as the senior partner of one of New York's largest law firms, and reports that he has never been happier.

Governor Dewey has frequently been recognized in academic circles for his contributions to public life. He has been awarded the Columbia Medal for Excellence, the Cardinal Newman Distinguished Service Award, and honorary degrees from the University of Michigan, Tufts College, Brown University, Dartmouth College, St. Lawrence University, New York University, Union College, Fordham University, Alfred University, Hamilton College, St. Bonaventure University, Colgate University, Williams College, Columbia University, Yeshiva University, and the University of Rochester.

While declining further public office, Thomas E. Dewey's activity in the public interest has never slackened. He takes a leading part in community responsibilities, and is frequently consulted by Republican leaders throughout the nation. He is presently serving as a member of the newly created, policy-formulating Republican Coordinating Committee.

J.A.W.